HOW TO:

SKYROCKET YOUR ONLINE GROWTH

BY CHASE CURTIS

Chase Curtis
www.buyrocketfuel.com

This book is dedicated to my wife & children.
For fueling me to be the best version of myself.

4

PROLOGUE

In the age of fleeting attention spans and the relentless barrage of digital information, the human desire for a space to collect, curate, and be inspired remains unchanged. Before the digital age, dream-boards—collages of aspirational images and quotes—found their way onto the walls of artists, planners, and dreamers. These tangible boards stood as beacons, reminders of goals, aspirations, and the beauty of the unseen and unexperienced.

Enter Pinterest. What started as a digital space for a few to pin their dreams transformed into a global phenomenon, reshaping the way millions seek inspiration. But Pinterest is not just another app on our phones or a fleeting trend on the digital horizon. It is the contemporary evolution of our intrinsic desire to dream, to plan, and to manifest.

This book is not just about using a platform. It's about tapping into this age-old desire, amplified by the power of technology. Whether you're a brand seeking visibility, a content creator desiring outreach, or simply a dreamer looking for your next big idea, this guide will take you on a journey. From understanding the heart of Pinterest to harnessing its full potential, get ready to pin your aspirations and watch them come to life.

Let's embark on this journey, one pin at a time.

6

1.
THE
INTRODUCTION

F ounded in March 2010 by Ben Silbermann, Paul Sciarra, and Evan Sharp, Pinterest's genesis was inspired by Ben's love for collecting as a child. But instead of collecting insects or stamps, he wanted people to collect ideas. And so, the concept of "pinning" was born.

The initial version of Pinterest was a closed beta, and invitations were needed to join. This exclusivity built intrigue and demand. As people began using Pinterest, they realized it wasn't just another photo-sharing app; it was a tool for discovery and inspiration.

By January 2012, Pinterest had hit the 10 million user milestone faster than any other standalone site in history. It was clear that Pinterest was more than just a trend; it was revolutionizing how people sought inspiration on the internet.

IMPORTANCE OF PINTEREST

Pinterest stands out today in the crowded social media arena for several reasons:

Visual Search Engine: Unlike most other platforms, Pinterest functions primarily as a visual search engine. People come here to search for ideas, from home décor to fashion, recipes to travel destinations. This intent-driven search behavior is a goldmine for brands and individuals looking to inspire or be discovered.

Planning and Inspiration: While platforms like Instagram or Snapchat capture the 'now,' Pinterest captures the 'what's next.' Users often plan their future on Pinterest, be it weddings, home renovations, or holiday meals.

High Purchase Intent: Studies have shown that Pinterest users often have a higher purchase intent compared to users on other social platforms. They are actively seeking inspiration for something they wish to do or buy.

WHO SHOULD USE PINTEREST & WHY?

Brands and Retailers: With users actively searching for products, it's an excellent platform for showcasing products. Brands can create inspirational content that leads to purchases.

Bloggers and Content Creators: Pinterest can drive a significant amount of traffic to blogs or websites. A single viral pin can boost site visits exponentially.

Artists and Creatives: For those looking to showcase portfolios, from photographers to DIY crafters, Pinterest provides an ideal platform.

Planners and Dreamers: Even if not for business, many users find value in planning events, dreaming about future travels, or curating personal style boards.

NOT A SOCIAL MEDIA PLATFORM

Pinterest isn't just another social media platform; it's a global community of dreamers, planners, and doers. As we navigate this book, you'll uncover the tremendous potential that lies within those digital pinboards and learn how to harness it for your personal or professional growth.

2.
SETTING THE FOUNDATION

V enturing into Pinterest for the first time as a brand is like entering a bustling digital marketplace. Each stall (or pin) offers something unique, beckoning visitors with vibrant visuals and promising ideas. Before setting up your own stall, it's crucial to understand the foundations of this platform. Let's begin your Pinterest journey by covering the basics.

CREATING A PINTEREST ACCOUNT

Starting on Pinterest is straightforward, but for large brands & businesses, some specific steps may be in order:

Sign Up: Visit Pinterest.com and click on "Sign up." For brands, it's recommended to sign up with a business email that's associated with your brand.

Provide Details: Fill in the necessary details, including your brand name, password, and other pertinent information.

Preferences: Pinterest will prompt you to select a few areas of interest. This will help tailor your feed initially, so choose topics related to your brand.

PERSONAL VS. BUSINESS ACCOUNT

Why opt for a business account when personal accounts seem simpler? Here's why:

Access to Analytics: Business accounts provide detailed insights into how your pins, boards, and current trends.

Rich Pins: These are enhanced pins that pull extra information right from your website, adding more context to your pin automatically. We will talk more about these later.

Advertising: Only business accounts can run ads or "Promoted Pins."

Professional Look: A business profile showcases your website link prominently on your profile.

Transitioning from a personal account to a business account is seamless, ensuring you don't lose any of your existing content.

ANATOMY OF A PINTEREST PROFILE

A Pinterest profile is more than just pins. It's a reflection of your brand's identity and ethos:

Profile Picture: Use a high-resolution logo or a brand-associated image. Ensure it's recognizable even in a smaller size. Try to avoid text if you can help it.

Bio: A concise, engaging bio can set the tone. Describe your brand and what followers can expect from your pins.

Boards: Think of them as categories, folders on your computer, or shelves in a store. Organize your pins into relevant boards for easier navigation.

Followers & Following: Just like other social platforms, you can follow and be followed. Engage with relevant brands, influencers, or pinners in your niche.

VERIFYING YOUR WEBSITE

By verifying your website on Pinterest, you achieve two things: authenticity and access to website analytics. The verification process involves:

Adding a Meta Tag: Go to the "Edit settings" option on your profile, find the "Claim" section, and enter your website URL. Pinterest will provide a meta tag for you to add to the HTML code of your website.

Uploading an HTML File: Alternatively, you can download an HTML verification file from Pinterest and upload it to your website's root directory.

Wait for Verification: Once you've added the meta tag or uploaded the HTML file, return to Pinterest and click "Submit." Verification typically happens instantly, but can take up to 72 hours.

3.
LEARNING THE AUDIENCE

W hile technical foundation is vital, equally important is understanding the vast, varied audience that populates Pinterest. Knowing who they are, what they seek, and how they behave can significantly influence your brand's strategy and content creation on the platform.

DEMOGRAPHICS & USER STATS

Global Reach: With nearly 450 million monthly active users, Pinterest has a diverse user base spanning multiple countries, with a significant presence in the U.S., UK, France, and Germany.

Gender Distribution: Historically, Pinterest leaned towards a female audience. While women still make up a significant percentage, the male user base is rapidly growing.

Age Groups: The majority of Pinterest users are between 18-34, but the platform sees regular activity from older age groups, highlighting its wide appeal.

ON-PLATFORM BEHAVIOR

Pinterest is all about discovery. Here's what users generally seek:

DIY & Crafts: One of the most popular categories, with users looking for inspiration for home projects.

Home Décor & Design: From minimalist bedrooms to boho living rooms, home décor is huge.

Fashion & Beauty: Outfit inspirations, beauty tutorials, and product recommendations are continually pinned and repinned.

Food & Recipes: New culinary adventures, from quick snacks to gourmet meals.

Travel: From dreamy destinations to travel tips, this category is bustling with pins.

Education & Information: Infographics, tutorials, and educational content have a significant presence.

Understanding the top categories gives brands a clearer idea of potential content strategies and where they might fit in.

THE POWER OF VISUAL SEARCH

Beyond Textual Queries: Pinterest's visual search tool allows users to search using images. A picture of a lamp, for example, can lead to pins showcasing similar lamps or associated décor ideas.

Lens: Pinterest's Lens tool lets users take photos of items and then find similar items or related ideas on the platform.

Shop the Look: This feature enables users to buy products directly from pins. For brands, it bridges the gap between inspiration and purchase.

4.
CRAFTING THE PERFECT PINS

Pins are the essence of Pinterest. They're the primary content pieces that users interact with, and for brands, they represent opportunities: opportunities to inspire, engage, and even convert. Crafting the perfect pin is an art, backed by some science. Let's dive into the nuances of creating pins that stand out and leave a lasting impact.

IMPORTANCE OF HIGH-RESOLUTION IMAGES

Crystal Clear Message: Blurry or pixelated images can be off-putting and reduce user engagement. High-resolution images convey professionalism and care for quality.

Zoom-In Feature: Pinterest users often zoom in to see details. Ensure your images remain sharp even when zoomed.

Trustworthiness: High-quality images tend to be perceived as more credible by users.

THE SCIENCE BEHIND VERTICAL PINS

Optimized for Mobile: Over 80% of Pinterest's traffic comes from mobile devices. Vertical pins take up more screen real estate, capturing more attention.

Aspect Ratio: Pinterest's recommended aspect ratio is 2:3, like 1000 x 1500 pixels. However, I prefer an aspect ratio of 3:4. This ensures that the pin looks good both on desktop and mobile.

Avoid Overly Long Pins: The tallest you can go with a pin is 900 x 1800. Any pin taller than this will be truncated.

TEXT OVERLAYS: TIPS AND TOOLS

Convey More Information: A well-placed text overlay can provide context to an image, making it more enticing for a click or save. Plus, Pinterest's algorithm is able to read on-pin text to enable faster search placement.

Readability: Use clear fonts that stand out against your image. Consider drop shadows, color gradients, or semi-transparent overlays if the background is busy.

Concise Messaging: Keep it short and sweet. Users should grasp the message in a split second.

Tools: Apps like Canva, PicMonkey, or Adobe Spark offer user-friendly platforms to add text overlays with ease.

BRAND CONSISTENCY ON PINTEREST

Logo Placement: Consider subtly adding your logo to pins. This ensures brand recognition without being overly promotional. I would go a step further and add your website to pins as well to ensure you receive some benefit if your pins are stolen.

Brand Presence: Use a consistent color scheme and font that reflects your brand's identity. It helps in building a recognizable and cohesive brand presence.

Tone & Voice: Whether it's the text overlay on the pin or the description accompanying it, maintain a consistent tone that aligns with your brand voice.

SCIENCE & ART INTERTWINED

Crafting the perfect pin is a blend of understanding the platform's technicalities and unleashing your creativity. Each pin is a canvas, an opportunity to tell a story, evoke an emotion, or spark an idea. And while trends on Pinterest will evolve, the underlying principle remains: authentic, high-quality content always finds its audience.

As we venture further, we'll delve into how to ensure these beautifully crafted pins reach the widest audience possible and resonate deeply with them.

5.
MAKING PINS DISCOVERABLE

The aesthetics of a pin play a pivotal role in capturing attention. Meanwhile, the behind-the-scenes optimization determines whether your pins reach your target audience. Just as SEO is to search engines, pin optimization is crucial for visibility on Pinterest. Let's unpack the essential elements to optimize every pin for maximum discoverability.

THE ROLE OF KEYWORDS ON PINTEREST

Keyword Research: Before creating pins, conduct keyword research using Pinterest's search bar and trends in your analytics. Note down frequently appearing terms related to your brand or content.

Pin Descriptions: Incorporate these keywords naturally into your pin descriptions. It makes your pins more likely to appear in relevant searches.

Board Titles & Descriptions: Don't just stop at pins. Infuse keywords into your board titles and descriptions for added optimization.

COMPELLING DESCRIPTIONS

Tell a Story: While it's tempting to just list keywords, weave them into a narrative or a compelling description. It should provide context and value to the viewer.

Call to Action: Encourage users to take action, whether it's visiting your website, trying a recipe, or buying a product.

Limit Length: While you have up to 500 characters, most users won't see beyond the first 50-60 on their feed. Make the beginning count!

USING HASHTAGS EFFECTIVELY

Pinterest & Hashtags: Unlike platforms like Instagram or Twitter, hashtags on Pinterest have been a relatively recent addition. They aid in content discovery, especially for fresh pins.

Relevance is Key: Only use hashtags that are directly related to your content.

Limit the Number: 3-5 well-chosen hashtags are generally more effective than a barrage of loosely related ones.

THE POWER OF RICH PINS

What are Rich Pins?: They provide more context about a pin by automatically pulling data from the linked website. There are four types: Product, Recipe, Article, and App pins.

Enhanced Visibility: Rich pins stand out more, offering users more information and a direct link to the source.

Setting Up: Ensure your website is verified on Pinterest [see the end of Chapter 2], and after approval, all pins linking to your site will be automatically enhanced.

How do they work?: Whenever a user shares your content on Pinterest or from your website or from a text to Facebook through email to Pinterest, your content will always link back to you.

Plus, the metadata for your content is pulled from your site, so you don't have to worry about any of the other items mentioned in this chapter. Do it right once on site, and everything else will be taken care for Pinterest.

6.
CURATING YOUR BOARDS

Imagine walking into an art gallery. Each room hosts a collection of paintings centered around a specific theme or narrative. Pinterest boards function similarly. They're themed collections where pins are curated, providing users with a structured browsing experience. As with everything on Pinterest, there's an art to organizing and curating these boards for maximum impact and brand coherence.

SETTING UP YOUR FIRST BOARDS

Start with Your Brand's Core Themes: If you're a fashion brand, you might have boards like "Summer Outfits," "Accessories Spotlight," or "Runway Inspirations."

Inspirational vs. Promotional: Not every board needs to directly promote products or services. Some can be purely for inspiration or to showcase the brand's values and aesthetics with other Pinner's content.

Easy Navigation: Name your boards clearly. Avoid jargon or overly creative titles that might confuse users. Starting off with 3-5 boards is ideal in your first few months, so you don't spread yourself too thin.

USING SECRET BOARDS

What Are They?: Secret boards are visible only to you (and those you invite). They won't appear publicly on your profile.

Content Planning: Use secret boards to plan pins or curate content before making them public. Secret boards are excellent for working with your team on platform.

Personal vs. Professional: You can also use secret boards for personal pins that you don't want to share with your audience but still want to save.

USING GROUP BOARDS

Collaborative Spaces: Group boards allow multiple pinners to contribute. They're a nice way for brands to collaborate with influencers, fans, or even team members.

Exposure Boost: By joining popular group boards relevant to your niche, you can expose your content to a wider audience.

Best Practices: Ensure the board has a clear focus. Set guidelines for contributors to maintain quality and coherence.

Are Group Boards Worth It?: In my experience, no. They're good for jumpstarting your growth, but most group boards only accept mature accounts.

BOARD COVERS AND AESTHETICS

First Impressions Count: The cover image of your board sets the tone. Choose a high-quality image that represents the board's content.

Consistency: Consider using a consistent style or color palette for all board covers to create a cohesive look on your profile.

Regular Updates: Periodically refresh board covers to reflect the evolving content or to align with seasonal themes.

THE POWER OF CURATION

In the vast sea of content, curation has emerged as a potent tool. By thoughtfully organizing and selecting pins for your boards, you're not just promoting products or services. You're telling a story, building an identity, and providing value to your followers. As you evolve and grow on Pinterest, continually revisit your boards. Refine, reorganize, and re-envision them to align with your brand's journey and your audience's needs.

7.
THE ART OF ENGAGEMENT

The true essence of Pinterest lies in fostering genuine connections. Engagement isn't just about boosting numbers; it's about creating meaningful interactions that resonate and leave a lasting impact. Let's delve into the art and science of engagement on this unique platform.

THE IMPORTANCE OF COMMUNITY

Value Beyond Pins: Users come to Pinterest for inspiration, ideas, and discovery, but they stay to build the life they've always dreamed of. Building a sense of community can amplify their experience and lead to returning users [and followers].

Trust and Authenticity: Regular engagement fosters trust, positioning your brand as genuine and authentic in the eyes of followers.

Feedback Loop: Engaging with your community provides valuable feedback, giving insights into user preferences and trends.

REPINNING: BEST PRACTICES

The Power of Shared Content: Repinning content from others, especially from users who engage with your brand, fosters a sense of community and recognition. This will get harder as your account grows, but is a great move from day one.

Quality Over Quantity: While repinning can boost engagement, ensure the content aligns with your brand's voice and aesthetic. Don't share spam or things that you wouldn't want tied to your brand.

Give Credit: Always acknowledge original creators. It's ethical and often appreciated by the original pinner. I would avoid using other people's pins/content like the plague, but there are accounts out there that thrive with aggregate content [after getting permission of course].

ENGAGING WITH COMMENTS

A Personal Touch: Responding to comments and messages, even if briefly, can make users feel valued. It's very rare to see users engaging at this level on Pinterest, so don't take it for granted.

Handle Criticism Gracefully: Not all feedback will be positive. Address negative comments with grace and professionalism.

Promptness Matters: Try to respond in a timely manner. The faster you engage, the fresher the interaction is in the user's mind.

COLLABORATION

Leverage Established Audiences: Collaborating with Pinterest influencers can introduce your brand to their followers, expanding your reach.

Genuine Partnerships: Seek partnerships that feel organic. Forced or mismatched collaborations can come off as inauthentic.

Collaborative Boards: Consider creating group boards where influencers can contribute, merging their audience with yours.

THE RIPPLE EFFECT

Engagement, when done right, creates momentum. Each comment, repin, or collaboration has the potential to exponentially increase your brand's visibility and impact. But beyond metrics, remember the human element. Each interaction is an opportunity to touch a life, inspire a mind, or foster a connection.

As your Pinterest journey unfolds, let engagement be the compass guiding your actions and decisions. Not as a mere strategy, but as an authentic commitment to enriching the lives of those who interact with your brand.

8.
GROWING YOUR ACCOUNT

Harnessing the platform's full potential requires consistent growth and expanding your reach. Growing your Pinterest profile means more eyes on your content, a larger community, and ultimately, a more robust impact for your brand. Let's dive into the strategies and nuances of effectively scaling your Pinterest presence.

PINNING CONSISTENTLY

Pinterest, like many other platforms, uses algorithms to show users new, relevant content. If you're pinning consistently, you're continually signaling to the platform that you're active and providing fresh content. This can increase the likelihood that your pins appear in more users' feeds.

Tailored Recommendations: Remember, Pinterest doesn't just show pins randomly. It recommends pins based on user behavior and preferences. By pinning consistently, you're increasing the odds that your content aligns with a user's specific interest at any given moment.

Consistency vs. Volume: It's worth noting that "consistency" doesn't always mean "high volume." Instead of flooding your profile with many pins at once, spread them out over time and set a minimum quality standard for the content you share. This ensures you won't be flagged by spam systems.

Pin Amounts: The suggested range of 5-15 pins a day is a good starting point, but frequency should be fine-tuned based on engagement metrics and specific audience behavior. Once you've found your groove. 30-50 new pins per day is ideal.

Quality over Quantity: Rather than just aiming for a certain number, focus on the quality of the pins. It's better to share 5 high-quality, engaging pins than 15 pins with little relevance or appeal.

Content Repurposing: If you're struggling to generate new content daily, consider repurposing your existing content. For instance, an old blog post can be transformed into 4-5 pins with different images, quotes, or headlines. Or ten of your similar products could be repurposed into an 'top list' and re-shared.

Pinning Your Content: There are two ways you can get your pins on Pinterest, and they both require human input. The best way to pin your content is directly from your site, but we will address this more in the second book.

CROSS-PROMOTION

Leverage Existing Channels: Promote your Pinterest profile on your website, newsletters, and other social media platforms. As Pinterest sends more traffic to your site, optimize your site to send that same traffic back into Pinterest.

Integrated Campaigns: Launch campaigns that run across multiple platforms, with Pinterest playing a specific role in the user journey.

Embed Pins: If you run a blog or website, embedding pins within your content can drive traffic to your Pinterest profile. Embedding your profile feed into your website sidebar is always a safe play.

USING WIDGETS AND PLUGINS ON YOUR WEBSITE

Save Button: Integrate the Pinterest Save button on your website images. This allows users to directly pin content to their boards.

Follow Button: A simple "Follow me on Pinterest" button can convert website visitors into Pinterest followers.

Board Showcase: Using plugins, display specific boards on your website, providing users a snapshot of your Pinterest content.

JOINING PINTEREST GROUP BOARDS

Community Engagement: Group boards are a congregation of like-minded pinners. Joining relevant boards significantly amplifies your reach to the combined count of everyone involved. While they were severely nerf'd in 2019, they can still be used to your advantage..

Finding Group Boards: Use tools like PinGroupie or simply use Pinterest search to find boards related to your niche. Then, reach out to the users that control the group board directly on Pinterest via direct message.

Contribute Value: Don't just use group boards for promotion. Add value by pinning content that aligns with the board's theme and resonates with its audience.

THE EVER-EVOLVING JOURNEY

Growing your Pinterest profile is not a one-time effort. It's an ongoing journey of learning, adaptation, and evolution. The platform, its algorithms, and user behaviors change over time.

Remember, growth on Pinterest, as with any platform, is not just about numbers. It's about the quality of interactions, the depth of engagements, and the genuine connections you foster outside of the platform.

9.

THE ANALYTICS

I t's easy to get lost in the aesthetic beauty of pins and boards. However, behind the scenes, there's an equally compelling narrative being told through numbers. Analytics serve as the compass guiding brands through the complex landscape of Pinterest, ensuring they're on the right path to achieving their goals. Let's unravel the story these numbers tell and how to leverage them effectively.

UNDERSTANDING PINTEREST ANALYTICS

Pinterest Analytics provides a holistic view of your profile's performance, audience demographics, and engagement metrics with three main categories:

Overview: Measures the performance of your pins, boards, and overall growth.

Audience Insights: Provides demographic information of your audience like interests, age, gender, and location.

Trends: Gives brands insight into what topics are growing this month, this year, seasonally, and more. New accounts can't afford to miss this.

KEY METRICS TO TRACK

Impressions: The number of times your pin appeared on someone's screen. It's a measure of visibility. In the beginning, this is the primary indicator of a successful pin and pinning strategy.

Saves (Re-pins): Indicates how many users found your pin valuable enough to save to their boards. This is the secondary indicator of a successful pin. Everything after impressions and saves is just a bonus.

Clicks: Reveals user interest, as they took the action to learn more about the pin. There is a different between a click for 'zooming in' and an outbound click, but both send a positive signal to the algorithm.

Engagement Rate: Calculated as engagements divided by impressions, it's a measure of how compelling your pins are.

Audience Growth: Tracks follower increase, helping gauge growth strategies' effectiveness.

ADJUSTING YOUR STRATEGY BASED ON DATA

Iterative Process: Use analytics to identify what's working and what's not. Tweak your strategy accordingly. If you have a pin blowing up organically, you should focus on creating more content around the same idea.

Content Refinement: If certain pins or board themes consistently underperform, consider re-evaluating your content approach or giving it time. A complete picture typically takes about 6 months to form.

Engagement Analysis: Low engagement rates might mean your pins aren't resonating. Consider changing visuals, descriptions, or keywords.

Optimal Posting Times: While the Pinterest platform definitely has peak user times, you won't ever really feel their effects until your account has amassed a few thousand followers. It's best to focus on consistent output rather than debating on posting at 7:15 or 7:45.

THIRD-PARTY ANALYTICS TOOLS

While Pinterest's in-built analytics is powerful, sometimes you might need deeper insights or specific features. Here are some third-party tools to consider:

Tailwind: Offers advanced scheduling features, detailed analytics, and insights into the best times to post.

Google Analytics: While not Pinterest-specific, you can track Pinterest referral traffic and user behavior on your site.

Note: I do not use any scheduling or third-party software outside of Google Analytics [as this data is required by advertisers], but they can play a critical role for individuals who like to batch their work.

10.
THE PAID ADVANTAGE

In the vast universe of Pinterest, where millions of pins vie for attention, standing out can be a challenge. While organic growth and engagement are essential and grow over time, there comes a point when brands seek an accelerated boost. In a world where you can pay-to-win, Pinterest is no different.

PINTEREST ADVERTISING

What are Promoted Pins?: Essentially, these are regular pins that you pay to display to a wider, targeted audience. Much like how you'd boost a post on Facebook or Twitter.

Visibility and Engagement: Promoted Pins not only boost visibility but can also increase engagement, driving actions like clicks, saves, and more.

Beyond Pins: Apart from pins, Pinterest offers other ad formats like Promoted Carousels, Promoted Video Pins, and Shopping Ads.

YOUR FIRST CAMPAIGN

Objective Selection: Define what you aim to achieve—brand awareness, engagement, traffic, app installs, or sales.

Targeting the Right Audience: Use Pinterest's detailed targeting options—demographics, interests, keywords, and more.

Ad Group Creation: Organize your promoted pins under ad groups, each with its unique budget and targeting.

Creative Choices: Ensure your pin design aligns with the campaign's objective. A sale-driven campaign may look different from a brand awareness campaign.

For Dummies: If you don't want to go through the hassle of managing ad campaigns, you can click on one of your top-performing pins and click the promote button at the top of page.

BUDGETING & TARGETING

Setting a Daily/Lifetime Budget: Decide how much you want to spend either daily or throughout the campaign's duration.

Bidding Strategy: Choose between automatic [Pinterest sets the bid] or manual [you set the bid] based on your budget and goals.

Audience Retargeting: Target users who've previously interacted with your brand, either on Pinterest or your website.

MEASURING ROI & SUCCESS METRICS

Defining Success: Depending on your campaign's objective, success might mean impressions, engagements, clicks, or actual sales.

Conversion Tracking: By installing the Pinterest tag on your website, you can track actions users take after viewing your promoted pin.

Optimizing for Better ROI: Regularly review campaign analytics. Adjust targeting, budgets, and creative elements for better returns.

Comparing Organic vs. Paid: Understand the difference in engagement and conversions between organic pins and promoted ones to gauge the true value of your ad spend.

BALANCE: ORGANIC & PAID

While promoted pins offer an undeniable advantage, it's crucial to maintain a balance.

A brand that solely relies on paid promotions may miss out on the authentic engagements and community building that organic growth fosters.

Conversely, solely banking on organic strategies may limit potential growth and visibility.

New accounts should focus less on the individual success of the promoted pin and more on the organic traffic you receive as a byproduct.

The first 30-90 days on Pinterest can be a drag. There's little-to-no movement, and the impressions you do receive are likely from browsing your own account. Boosting one or two pins for a few dollars per day will increase your organic growth dramatically.

If $500 could put you three months ahead, would you do it?

11.
THE RECAP

Out of all the useful information in this book, these are the gold nuggets you don't want to miss. Whenever you feel uncertain about the strategy or need a refresher, this is the place to go.

Impressions are everything. Saves, clicks, and engagements are all nice, but you're trying to grow - not thrive [yet].

The only way to speed up the process is to promote your pins. Pinterest is one of the few platforms where your ad money doesn't vanish into thin air when your campaigns end. Promoted pins can increase organic growth drastically, and any alternate opportunity that offers faster growth, that isn't paying for ads, likely won't work.

Fresh pins are vital for growth. Repinning your old pins may give you a small boost, but this it has its' limits. If you want to continue growing at an exponential pace, you need to be sharing brand new pins. Ideally 20-30 per day.

Rich Pins will save you mucho time. As soon as you can activate them, you need to do so. You will never have to manually upload a pin or edit details again. Anytime you want to adjust the pin, you change the info on your site and the pin will auto-pull the data.

Creating content based on data is better than creating content at random. On day one, you can create whatever you feel like, but by day 30, you should have enough analytical data to make an informed decision on what niche or topic you need to focus on.

The trends page in your analytics is your new best friend. If you don't want to start from a point of uncertainty, use the trends page to learn what happens on Pinterest like clockwork. What was popping off last year? What seasonal keywords do numbers? The trends page is your answer.

Every piece of content you create should have, at minimum, 3 low-effort and 1 high-effort Pinterest-optimized images. You're only cheating yourself out of growth if you aren't pin-stacking your content. I shoot for 5 images per piece regardless of niche or topic. However, I wouldn't go over 10 images as this could potentially create a poor user experience.

Craft one max-length image per post/product. A pin that is 900x1800 will fill the max amount of screen real estate without being cut off. It's best to use these pins for infographics, providing context [like text & CTAs], or creating a visual collage from your low-effort images.

You should dedicate 30-minutes per day to using the platform like a normal user. Yes, you should still be logged into your brand's business account when doing so, but by engaging with the platform like a real user, you send positive signals to the algorithm. Sharing 30-50 fresh pins per day is good. Sharing 30-50 fresh pins per day and repining 30-50 pins from other users is better.

Starting with 3 boards is enough. One board dedicated to solely your content, one board pinning other's content, and one board to mixing your content and their content together. This will also make it easier for you to find your older pins if you need them.

Brand visuals need to remain consistent. Once users identify your brand as high value, being able to quickly distinguish your work in the feed is infinitely beneficial. Use the same font, the assets, and the notable colors.

Top-performing pins should fuel your content creation. The longer you're on the platform, the easier it will be to develop an idea of what your audience is interested in. Take your pins with the highest impressions and saves to ChatGPT, and ask it to generate similar ideas to the top-performing content.

Encourage your web visitors to share via Pinterest. Getting a new account off the ground can be challenging, especially if you aren't getting your daily reps in. You can download plugins that add a Pinterest 'share button' to every image on your site, and this can work wonders in building initial traction.

Relax. This system takes time. Nearly every platform today rewards you instantaneously for your content, and then it disappears in a content black hole for... forever. You may not reap the benefits of your actions for a month [or six], but when your pins start hitting - they hit hard.

12.
NOTES

As you journeyed through the pages of this book, I'm certain you've encountered insights, revelations, and moments of epiphany. To assist you in capturing these invaluable takeaways, I've dedicated this section to you - a blank canvas for your thoughts, ideas, statistics, and reflections.

DON'T FORGET THE GOOD STUFF

Over the next 50 pages, allow your mind to wander and your pen to run free. Whether it's a statistic that challenged your perspective or a spontaneous idea birthed from your reading, let nothing escape uncaptured.

Remember, sometimes our greatest inspirations come in the quiet moments of reflection.

Happy jotting!